CONTENTS

INTRODUCTION TO AUSTRALIA

Clues from place names

The names of places in Australia can tell us a lot about Australia's history. Names, such as Wagga Wagga and Uluru, are reminders that the first Australians were the **aboriginal people**. They may have arrived between 50,000 and 100,000 years ago when there was no sea between Australia and Asia.

Some places, such as Newcastle and Perth, are named after British towns. Adelaide and Victoria are named after British queens, and the city of Melbourne takes its name from a British Prime Minister, Viscount Melbourne.

Ancient rock paintings drawn by aboriginal people.
- *The paintings often show animals and sometimes hands and feet.*
- *These are sacred places to the aboriginal people.*

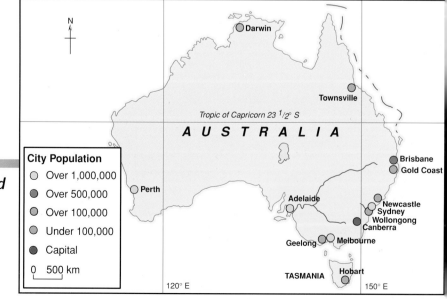

Australia: towns and population.

City Population
- ○ Over 1,000,000
- ● Over 500,000
- ○ Over 100,000
- ○ Under 100,000
- ● Capital

0   500 km

N

Darwin

Townsville

Tropic of Capricorn 23 1/2° S

AUSTRALIA

Perth

Brisbane
Gold Coast

Adelaide

Newcastle
Sydney
Wollongong
Canberra

Geelong   Melbourne

TASMANIA   Hobart

120° E   150° E

Australia

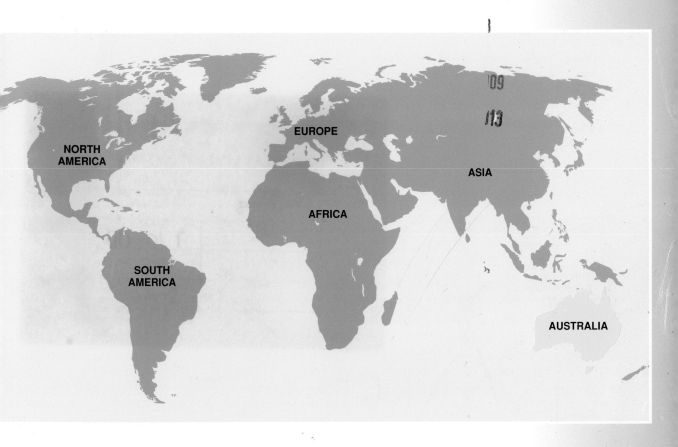

NORTH AMERICA

EUROPE

ASIA

AFRICA

SOUTH AMERICA

AUSTRALIA

'09

/13

Fred Martin

First published in Great Britain by Heinemann Library
Halley Court, Jordan Hill, Oxford OX2 8EJ
a division of Reed Educational and Professional Publishing Ltd

Heinemann is a registered trademark of Reed Educational and Professional Publishing Ltd

OXFORD FLORENCE PRAGUE MADRID ATHENS
MELBOURNE AUCKLAND KUALA LUMPUR SINGAPORE TOKYO
IBADAN NAIROBI KAMPALA JOHANNESBURG GABORONE
PORTSMOUTH NH (USA) CHICAGO MEXICO CITY SAO PAULO

Designed by AMR
Illustrations by Art Construction
Printed in Hong Kong / China

03 02 01 00 99
10 9 8 7 6 5 4 3 2 1

ISBN 0 431 01374 8

British Library Cataloguing in Publication Data

Martin, Fred, 1948-
  Australia. – (Next Stop)
  1. Australia – Geography – Juvenile literature
  I.Title
  919.4

This book is also available in hardback (ISBN 0 431 01373 X).

Acknowledgements
The Publishers would like to thank the following for permission to reproduce photographs:
Aspect Pictures, Derek Bayes, p.25, John Earrett, p.23, Alex Langley, p.14; Colorific Photo Library, Bill Bachman, p.6, Philip Hayson, p.26, Penny Tweedie, p.19, Barbara Wale, p.4, David Young, p.18; J. Allan Cash, p.11; Panos Pictures, Penny Tweedie, pp.9, 27, 28; Still Pictures, Mark Edwards, pp.15, 22, Klein/Hubert, pp.7, 8, Gerald and Margi Moss, pp.5, 10; Trip Photo Library, R. Nichols, p.24, Eric Smith, pp.12, 13, 16, 17, 21, 29.

Cover photographs: Zefa and Gareth Boden

Every effort has been made to contact holders of any material reproduced in this book. Any omissions will be rectified in subsequent printings if notice is given to the Publisher.

The cove where Captain James Cook began the settlement of Sydney.
- *The high rise buildings are in the centre of Sydney's city centre.*
- *The building with the unusual roof is the Sydney Opera House.*

Early exploration

Europeans did not know about Australia until explorers, such as Willem Jansz and Abel Tasman, sailed through the area in the seventeenth century. The first European to set foot on the Australian mainland was Captain James Cook in 1770, when he landed at Botany Bay on the east coast. Then on 26 January 1788 he sailed into nearby Port Jackson where he started the settlement of Sydney. Australia's national day is 26 January.

At first, Britain used Australia as a place to send convicts. They were sent to **penal colonies**. Sydney was one of these penal colonies. No more convicts were sent after 1868. By then, Australia was also important for rearing sheep and for gold mining. Thousands of people **emigrated** to Australia from Britain to escape from poverty and to start new lives. By 1901, Australia had become an **independent country**.

A growing country

People continued to migrate to Australia during the 20th century, mainly from the UK and other European countries. More recently, migrants have come from Asian countries, such as Vietnam and Malaysia. The country's population is now just over eighteen million. Of these, four out of every ten are either migrants, or the sons or daughters of migrants.

The Australian national anthem is called *Advance Australia Fair*. The flag includes a Union Jack to show its links with the UK. The flag has six stars. Five are in the form of the Southern Cross constellation which is seen in the sky over the southern hemisphere. The sixth star is the largest and has seven points, each representing a state or territory. Australia's national colours are green and gold.

THE NATURAL LANDSCAPE

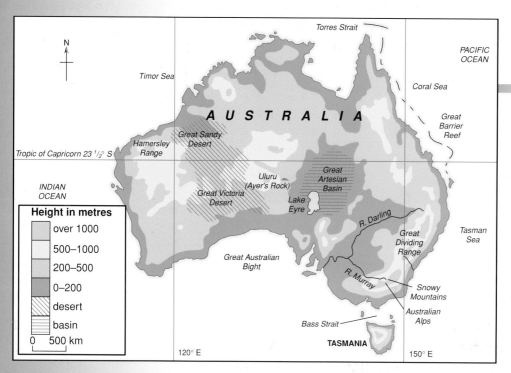

Australia: natural features.

Height in metres	
	over 1000
	500–1000
	200–500
	0–200
	desert
	basin
0 500 km	

The smallest continent

Australia is about 4000 km from east to west and about 3700 km from north to south. Australasia includes the **continent** of Australia, New Zealand and some other nearby islands.

Most of Australia's landscape consists of lowland **plains** that are flat or have low hills. The rocks are some of the earth's oldest, and are up to about five billion years old. Geologists call an area like this a **shield**.

Basins and lakes

There are not many rivers in the central parts of Australia because there is so little rain. Most rivers and small streams dry up for several months each year.

A scene in the plains of Australia.
- *Rivers and water holes often dry up.*
- *One way to round up the cattle is by motorbike.*

However, there is water in **artesian basins** in the rocks deep underground. Some of this water has trickled down through the rocks, from mountains in wetter areas hundreds of kilometres away. Farmers get this water for their animals by drilling deep boreholes and using wind or motor pumps. Most of it is too salty for people to drink.

Lake Eyre is Australia's biggest lake with an area of 9475 square kilometres (km²). Most of the streams and rivers that enter it are completely dry for several months each year and sometimes for several years at a time. This means the lake often dries out and becomes a salt marsh. It quickly fills and gets bigger when there is rain. No rivers flow out of Lake Eyre. This is because it is an area of **inland drainage**. It is in a giant hollow that is fourteen metres below sea level.

Australia's mountains

The highest mountain peaks are in the Great Dividing Range in the east. Mountain ranges, such as the Snowy Mountains and the Australian Alps, are part of this larger range. The Murray river, which flows west from the Snowy Mountains, is Australia's longest river. It keeps flowing because of melting winter snow and because it is joined by tributary rivers such as the Darling and Murrumbidgee.

One of Australia's most spectacular **landforms** is called Uluru, or Ayer's Rock. Uluru is a huge 348 metre high sandstone rock, called a **monolith**, that rises almost vertically above the surrounding flat desert floor. The sunlight gives it a different colour at different times of the day.

The interior part of Australia, away from the towns and the coast, is known as the outback.

Australia's famous landmark.
- *Tourists come to the outback to see Uluru (Ayer's Rock).*
- *This scene is at sunrise.*
- *At sunset, the colour of the rock can change to red.*

CLIMATE, VEGETATION AND WILDLIFE

A forest with eucalyptus trees.
- *Eucalyptus trees are also called gum trees.*
- *This forest is in the state of Victoria.*
- *There are not many forests like this left.*

Desert and monsoon

Australia is the world's driest **continent**, apart from Antarctica. About one-third of Australia is a **hot desert** where the total annual rainfall is less than 250 mm. To the north and east of the deserts, there is a **savanna climate** with two distinct seasons. One is hot and wet and the other is warm and dry. The rainfall each year, however, is very unreliable and there is **drought** in some years.

The wettest areas, with at least 1000 mm of rain, are in the north and east where there is a **tropical monsoon climate**. Much of the rain comes from hot monsoon winds that blow from the north in February and March. Typhoons sometimes strike the north and north east coasts.

Most Australians live in the south east where the climate is like that around the Mediterranean Sea. It is hot and dry in summer and mild and wetter in winter.

Plants and animals

The type of natural vegetation depends mainly on the climate. There is scrub in the deserts. Grasslands and scattered trees are found in the savanna areas, and there are also areas of tropical and temperate rain forests. Different types of eucalyptus or gum trees are typical in the south east. Australia's national flower is the golden wattle which is a type of acacia.

Many species of Australia's wildlife are unique to the country. This is because Australia broke away from a much larger continent millions of years ago. The animals developed in different ways from those in other parts of the world.

The kangaroo is an animal that is only found in Australia. It is a **marsupial**, which is an animal with a pouch where it rears its young, which are called joeys. Some of Australia's other animals include koalas, wombats, crocodiles, poisonous spiders, snakes and termites. There are also flightless emus and birds such as cockatoos and budgerigars.

Off the north east shores of Australia is the Great Barrier Reef. It looks like rock, but has been made by tiny creatures called coral polyps.

Conserving Australia's remaining wildlife and plants is a huge task. Even the Great Barrier Reef is under threat from pollution and from too many people visiting it.

The duck-billed platypus is one of Australia's most unusual animals. Its mouth is like a duck's beak and it also lays eggs, but it is not a bird. It has fur and it feeds its young on milk. It is a very strange mammal.

TOWNS AND CITIES

The 'bush capital'

Almost nine out of every ten people in Australia live in towns and cities. This is more than in almost any other country. Most Australian people live in the big cities in the east and south east, such as Brisbane, Sydney and Melbourne. Perth in Western Australia and Adelaide in South Australia are two other main cities.

Canberra is Australia's **capital city**. It is sometimes called the 'bush capital' because it is surrounded by dry bush landscape. The site for Canberra was chosen in 1908. The city has an artificial lake and broad main streets with geometric shapes. It is home to the national parliament, law courts, foreign embassies and other important national buildings. New towns have been built in the surrounding countryside since 1960.

The Sydneysiders

Sydney is Australia's main shipping port, industrial and business centre and the biggest city in every way. It covers an area of 1800 square kilometres and has a population of 3.7 million. Just over one in every five Australians is a Sydneysider. The central business district is linked to **suburbs** on the north shore of Sydney Harbour by the Sydney Harbour bridge. Inland, the city stretches out on the flat valley land of the Hawkesbury and other rivers.

The city of Sydney is Australia's biggest city.
- *High-rise buildings show the main business and shopping centre.*
- *The harbour is used by ships and small yachts.*
- *Areas of housing stretch out from the city centre.*

10

There are many opportunities for recreation in and near Sydney. People can visit the Blue Mountains and other national parks, swim and surf on the famous Bondi Beach and sail in the harbour's sheltered waters. The Olympic Games will be held in Sydney in the year 2000.

Special characters

Australia's other main cities each have their own special character. The oldest buildings are usually churches and houses from the first half of the nineteenth century. More recent suburbs spread out into the countryside.

Alice Springs is the only large town in the outback. It was built as a service centre for people who live on farms in the surrounding area. Tourism is now becoming important in Alice Springs, even though it is so far from the major towns and cities. Some of Australia's other outback towns were built as mining settlements. Mount Tom Price, for example, was built for miners in iron ore quarries. They live there with their families.

The city of Melbourne.
- *The busy Bourke Street shopping mall.*
- *There is a mix of old and new buildings.*
- *A tram service links the city centre to the outer suburbs.*

Coober Pedy in South Australia is one of Australia's most unusual settlements. The town is a centre for mining opals. Just under half the people live in underground houses to get away from the heat. The town's name comes from *aboriginal* words that mean 'man who lives in a hole'.

SYDNEY'S SUBURBS

The family home.
- *Sitting outside the family home in St Ives, a suburb of Sydney.*
- *This scene is in July, in the middle of the Australian winter.*

The family home

The suburbs of Sydney stretch out into land that used to be farmland with villages. The suburb of St Ives is a residential area about 20 kilometres to the north of the city centre. This is where the Rich family live.

There are five people in the family. The parents are Geoffrey and Jane and their children are Graeme aged thirteen, Katie aged ten and Jenna aged seven. Unlike many Australians, everyone in the family was born in Australia and they have always lived in the same area. They live in a two-storey detached house built from brick and wood. The family can sit outside in the shade of a veranda. There is a garden with grass, flowers and trees. There is also a big swimming pool in the garden.

The neighbourhood.
- *The neighbourhood has many trees with plenty of space for each house.*
- *There is not much traffic in a residential area such as St Ives.*

The neighbourhood is a pleasant area with good roads, trees and a good range of services. There is a new shopping centre with a supermarket and other shops. There is parkland where people can relax and play games.

Work and school

Geoffrey works as a barrister in Sydney. The nearest station is only 3 kilometres from his home so he usually travels to work by train. The children all go to schools in the local area. Their parents drive them to school. Katie enjoys art and working with computers. She studies German as a foreign language. Reading is Jenna's favourite subject.

Enjoying life

Everyone in the family is very active in different kinds of sports, especially playing tennis. Geoffrey and son Graeme both play cricket. Geoffrey sometimes goes skiing. Jane goes swimming and coaches a softball team. Both Katie and Jenna also play softball. Katie is learning to play the flute. Jenna goes to ballet lessons and is also learning to play the piano. For family holidays, they usually go to a beach resort, to the country or they go **bushwalking**. The family enjoy living in a part of Australia where there are good opportunities for both work and recreation.

Playing sport.
- *Katie playing softball in the park in St Ives.*
- *Sport is taken seriously in Australia.*

Jane does most of the shopping in a supermarket in St Ives.

Jenna at work in her primary school.

FARMING

Sheep stations

There are at least eight times as many sheep as people in Australia. **Merino sheep** were brought from South Africa to Australia in the nineteenth century. Fine wool still earns money for Australia. About one-third of Australia is used for grazing sheep, although the wool now earns just under ten per cent of Australia's money from **exports**. The biggest sheep farms are in the dry grassland areas. They are called **sheep stations**.

The wool from the sheep is sheared by gangs of shearers who move from one sheep station to another. A good shearer can shear about 95 sheep in one day. The fleece has to be shorn in one piece to have the greatest value.
A general farm worker is called a **rouseabout**.

Outback cattle

There are also more cattle in Australia than people. There are about 22 million cattle, about half of them in the northern state of Queensland. Cattle in Queensland are bred for their meat. Dairy cattle are mainly farmed in the south east where grass grows better. These farms are also nearer to the cities where people want fresh milk.

Shearing sheep on a farm in South Australia.
- *Shearing is done by teams of shearers who travel from farm to farm.*
- *There are competitions for shearing to see who can shear the fastest.*
- *The record weight for one fleece is 29.5 kg from a Merino sheep in South Australia.*

A wheat farm in Western Australia.
- *The field, called a paddock, is so big that the boundaries are out of sight.*
- *Combine harvesters are used to do the work.*
- *There is a risk that farming will cause soil erosion in dry areas.*

Some outback cattle stations are bigger than UK counties. The cattle graze in the wild until they need to be rounded up. The farmers do this on horseback, on motorbikes or by helicopter. Using a helicopter is the quickest way to find the cattle.

Growing crops

Some Australian farmers grow wheat and other grain crops, such as maize and barley. The warm climate suits these crops but there must be enough rain or **irrigation** water to make them grow. Sugar cane is grown in the wet tropical north east. Grapes and fruits, such as peaches, are grown in the south east.

Dams and reservoirs have been built to help supply the farms with water. Farmers face other problems, such as wild dogs called dingoes that kill sheep. To stop them, a wire fence called the dog fence has been built for about 5300 km across Australia. Rabbits and kangaroos are also pests to farming. They eat grass and help cause **soil erosion**. It is hard to keep their numbers under control.

Rabbits were first brought to Australia in 1788 as part of Captain Cook's expedition. In 1859, 24 rabbits were released into the wild so they could be hunted for sport. The number living wild is now about 300 million. This is despite millions having been killed.

A FARMING FAMILY

At home on the farm

Travel west for about 320 km from Sydney. The journey takes you over the Blue Mountains to a landscape of open countryside on rolling hills. This is where the Reid family have their farm. The nearest town is Cowra which is a country town with about 8500 people. The Reid's farm is about 40 km from Cowra.

Chris and Elizabeth (Libby) Reid have four children. There is Prudence aged fifteen, James aged thirteen, Anna aged nine and Tobias (Toby) aged seven. Their house, built from granite blocks, has five bedrooms. There is a veranda around the house to give shelter from the summer sun. Drinking water comes from a tank on the roof that collects rainwater. Water for the garden comes from a nearby river. There is electricity for heat, light and cooking.

The local landscape.
- *The rolling hill landscape near Cowra.*
- *Farmers rear herds of sheep and cattle in the open farmland.*

The family house.
- *The Reid family outside their family home.*
- *The veranda helps give some shade.*

At the stock market.
- Chris Reid at a sheep market in Cowra.
- The sheep are mostly the **Merino** breed that are reared for their wool.

A family meal.
- Sitting down to dinner in the Reid's home.
- The family eat some foods they grow themselves and some that they buy in the shops in Cowra.

Country living

The farm is about 1900 hectares in size. This is very large compared to most farms in the UK. Most farmers in the area rear sheep and cattle. Some crops, including cereals and vines, are also grown. The Reid family have herds of about 8000 sheep and 400 cattle. Chris does most of the farm work, though Libby and the children often help as well.

The farm is isolated from other buildings and people. Libby travels to Cowra where she works as an accountant and where she does the shopping. The family also eat lamb, beef and some other produce from their own farm. Anna and Toby go to school in Cowra. Prudence and James go to a boarding school in Sydney. Their parents have to pay fees for them to go to this school.

Hobbies and interests

Chris has an interest in the wine industry, old sports cars and rugby. Libby enjoys looking after the garden. The children have a tree house where they play together. In summer, they go swimming in the nearby river. The family usually go on holiday to the coast. Most of all, they enjoy living in an area with so much open space and having the freedom to roam around it.

Anna in class.

SHOPS AND SERVICES

EXIT ONLY

WEST END

Buying drinks.
- *A drive-in shop selling drinks.*
- *Drive-in shops are mostly for food and drinks.*

Australian city shopping

Most Australians have a good standard of living. They have enough money to afford a wide variety of goods and services.

Shopping in cities, such as Sydney and Melbourne, is like shopping in any of the world's richest countries. There are department stores and supermarkets in the city centres. There are also smaller **speciality shops** for goods, such as clothes and jewellery. Shopping malls and arcades have been built in the city centres and in the **suburbs**. There are some street markets, but Australians do most of their shopping in the shops.

Many Australians have to drive a long way to do their shopping. This means the shopping areas must have good car parks. Food and drinks are sometimes sold from 'drive-ins'. Shops are usually open all day with late opening on at least one evening. Many shops are closed on Sundays. Shops often have overhead canopies to provide shade.

Outback services

Access to shops and services for people in the outback is very different. It may be a hundred kilometres or more to the nearest shop, or even to the nearest neighbour. Many farmers own light aircraft to get about and to do the shopping. They sometimes stock up with food for several months. People on farms are also in contact with each other by radio and now by computers. Goods can be ordered through the post from mail order companies.

Flying doctors

Access to services, such as doctors, is a special problem in remote areas. There is no time to lose when there is an emergency. The Flying Doctor service covers an area of six million square kilometres. It aims to get to anyone in no more than 90 minutes.

There are thirteen Flying Doctor bases throughout Australia, with a fleet of 38 light aircraft. They fly out and treat about 150,000 people every year. The patients are usually on outback farms, mining camps or other settlements that are too small to have their own doctor.

Australia has a School of the Air that broadcasts lessons to children who cannot get to a school because they are too far away. Some children go to boarding schools.

Help from the Flying Doctor.
- *The Flying Doctor service gets emergency help to the most remote places in the outback.*
- *The aircraft have to use short, bumpy landing strips.*

FOOD, OLD AND NEW

Hunting for food

The Australian **aborigines** learnt how to live off the land by hunting, fishing and collecting berries and eggs. These traditional wild foods are called 'bush tucker'. Aborigines hunted by using boomerangs to throw at wild animals, such as birds and wallabies. The boomerang's flat curved shape made it fly then return to the thrower if it missed the target. Spears were used to kill larger animals, such as kangaroo. Some aborigines who live in outback areas still hunt in this way but most now live on farms or in cities.

Changing habits

Many Australian dishes originally came from the UK. These included roast dinners with potatoes and vegetables. People also enjoy eating meat pies and fish and chips. Lamb and beef are plentiful because they are reared on Australian farms. People can also buy kangaroo and crocodile steaks in the shops and in restaurants. A traditional Christmas dinner is roast turkey, stuffing, vegetables and plum pudding. Lamingtons are small sponge cakes made from cocoa, icing sugar and coconut.

Barbecue.
- *The warm dry weather for much of the year is ideal for barbecues.*
- *A barbecue can be an occasion to entertain friends.*

Eating in a Greek taverna in Australia.
- *Immigrants have brought foods from many different countries to Australia.*
- *Now everyone can enjoy a wider range of foods.*

But now, Australians are eating a much wider variety of foods. This is mainly because of migration from countries including Italy, Greece and the Asian countries. A meal of pasta or a stir-fry is as popular as a traditional English dish. Hamburger restaurants are as common as in other rich countries.

There are many new dishes using tropical fruits, such as mango, avocado, pawpaw, banana and pineapple, grown in Australia. These are combined with more traditional foods to make both salads and cooked meals. Different types of fish such as freshwater lobsters called yabbies, prawns and a freshwater fish called barramundi are also popular.

The barbecue meal

Cooking in the open air on a barbecue is a popular way to prepare food, especially when entertaining friends. In many places, the warm weather throughout the year means that barbecues can be enjoyed at any time.

Australia is famous for its beers. Fosters and XXXX are two beers that are sold in countries all over the world. Australian wines, both red and white, have also become popular in Australia and in other countries as well.

Desserts such as Peach Melba and Pavlova are special Australian dishes. Pavlova is made from meringue with cream, passionfruit and other fruits. The name comes from a Russian ballet dancer. Peach Melba is named after an Australian opera singer called Dame Nellie Melba.

MINING AND INDUSTRY

Minerals and energy

Most of Australia is dry and barren, but the rocks beneath this landscape have some of the world's most valuable deposits of metals, such as iron, copper, gold and uranium. The Pilbara region in Western Australia has mountains that are rich in iron ore. There are deposits of bauxite in Queensland and other places. Bauxite is used to make aluminium. Some of these **raw materials** are used to make goods in Australian factories. The rest are exported to countries that need them, such as Japan and the UK.

Energy for Australia's industry and homes comes from its own deposits of coal, oil and natural gas. Some comes from hydro-electric power stations, such as those in the Snowy Mountains.

Mechanical diggers working to mine bauxite.
- *The natural forest is destroyed by the mining.*
- *The mining company has promised to restore the land when mining has finished.*

Industrial goods

About fifteen per cent of Australian workers work in **manufacturing industries**.

The main manufacturing industries are in the cities, such as Sydney, Melbourne and Adelaide. They make cars, chemicals, iron and steel and machinery. These are called **heavy industries**. There are also factories making **consumer goods,** such as clothes and electrical equipment. These are examples of **light industries**.

Australia's farms supply the raw materials for industries including those spinning wool and processing food. Peaches and other fruits are canned in Australia so they can be exported without going rotten.

Grapes grown in southern and eastern Australia are made into wine. In the Barossa Valley in South Australia there are at least 50 wineries. Wines from these wineries are sold in supermarkets throughout the UK. Australia also has a brewing industry that makes beer and lager.

Wilderness resources

Some of Australia's mineral resources are on land that the **aboriginal people** say is theirs. They want a share in the wealth from mining, but they are also afraid that mining will destroy their sacred sites. The Australian government now agrees that some of these lands should be given back.

Mineral resources have been found in some of Australia's most important **wilderness areas,** such as the Kakadu National Park in Northern Territory. It is difficult to take decisions about whether to use the land for quarrying or to conserve it for the future.

The art of making wine was brought to the Barossa Valley in 1842 by immigrants from Germany. The Barossa Valley was named after the Barossa sherry making region in Spain.

The vineyards of southern Australia.
- *Grapes are grown where there is a Mediterranean climate.*
- *The grapes are taken to a winery where they are crushed to make wine.*
- *Australian wine is made using the most modern methods and equipment.*

TRANSPORT

Continental scales

Australians have to travel **continental**-scale distances between cities. It takes 65 hours 45 minutes to travel the 2500 km between Sydney and Perth by train. The flight is faster but still takes 4 hours 35 minutes. It takes 92 hours by train, or a five-hour flight, to go from Sydney to Darwin in the north west.

Trains and aeroplanes

There are not many railway links between places in Australia. The few there are have special names, such as the overnight *Vinelander* and daytime *Sunraysia* trains between Melbourne and Mildura. Millions of tonnes of minerals are moved from quarries to ports on the coast, using specially-built **mineral lines**.

There are regular flights between the main cities on a 150,000 km network of air routes. There are about 240 airports with hard surface runways, but hundreds more with only a landing strip beside a farm building. Uluru (Ayer's Rock) has its own landing strip for visitors.

A road train.
- *Road trains are up to 50 metres long and may have 80 wheels.*
- *They transport cattle from cattle stations in Northern Territory and Queensland.*
- *The truck drivers must be able to drive in very hot weather and sometimes on poor roads.*

Sydney's monorail.
- *A monorail runs through Sydney's city centre.*
- *The monorail is a type of public transport that makes good use of space.*
- *The monorail helps take traffic off the roads.*

On and off road

There is at least one car to almost every family. Four out of every ten families have two cars and one in ten has three. Most journeys, including those carrying **freight**, are made by road. In the past, herds of cattle were driven by stockmen on horseback from remote cattle stations to city markets. Now they are taken by road trains. These are powerful trucks that pull two or more trailers. The cattle get to market much faster and without losing so much weight, or dying on the way.

Driving in the outback needs special care because of the long distances and the climate. Drivers are advised to carry spare cans of petrol and water because there are not many petrol stations. Anyone driving off the main roads needs a four-wheel drive vehicle to cope with bumpy unpaved tracks. Driving in the wet season can be hazardous because of sudden **flash floods**.

People travel in cities by car, bus, **suburban** trains and other types of public transport. A monorail runs around the central part of Sydney. In Melbourne, there are trams on the surface and electric trains underground.

The Sydney to Perth rail route crosses a flat desert area called the Nullarbor *Plain*. There is one 500 km stretch across the desert that is the longest stretch of straight railway line anywhere in the world. The plain gets its name from Latin words that mean 'no trees'.

SPORT AND LEISURE

A sporting nation

About 6.5 million Australians are members of sports clubs. This is about one in three of all the people in the country. Many of them play outdoor sports such as rugby, cricket and tennis. The warm and often dry climate gives good conditions for these sports throughout the year.

Australian cricket fans always want their team to win test matches for 'the Ashes' against England. Australia's rugby union and rugby league teams are among the best in the world. The rugby union team is called the 'Wallabies'. Football is played under Australia's own rules. In tennis, Rod Laver, Margaret Court, Evonne Cawley and Pat Cash have been top world players.

Water sports.
- *A competition between lifesavers in their boats at a beach near Sydney.*
- *The coast in this part of Australia is good for surfing and other water sports.*

There is snow in the highest mountains in south east Australia so skiing has become a popular sport. Mount Hotham, which is 1850 metres high, attracts skiers to its snow-covered slopes.

Beaches and oceans

Most Australians have easy access to the coast because most main cities are near the sea. Swimming, surfing and sailboarding are seen both as sports and as popular forms of recreation. The Great Barrier Reef is a favourite place for scuba diving and snorkelling.

Australians are also interested in yacht-racing. One of the main yacht races is the annual Sydney to Hobart (in Tasmania) race. Yachts on 'round the world' races usually stop for supplies at Australian ports. The sheltered waters of Sydney Harbour are ideal for people who prefer to sail in safety.

Outback trails

For most Australians, visiting the outback is like visiting another country. It is a wilderness where life is nothing like life in the cities. Wildlife – including crocodiles – lives in the rivers and swamplands of Northern Territory. Tourists travel to see spectacular natural sights, such as Uluru (Ayer's Rock) near the centre of Australia and canyons, such as St Katherine's Gorge in the far north. White-water rafting and canoeing are also popular.

Some people prefer to get away from the crowds and go **bushwalking**. Australia is certainly big enough to get away from the crowds.

In 1997, the tennis player Mark Philippousis broke the world record for the fastest serve. His new record was to make the tennis ball travel at 232 km/h (144 mph).

Outback leisure.
- *Walking and camping in the bush is a growing leisure activity.*
- *This scene is in the bush landscape of Western Australia.*

ARTS, CULTURE, CUSTOMS

Dreamtime arts

The **aboriginal people** have lived in Australia for at least the last 50,000 years. Over this time, they have developed their own beliefs, customs and art. Traditional aboriginal beliefs describe a **dreamtime** when spirits in the shape of different animals lived on the earth. Features in the landscape were made by these animals. River valleys for example, were made by a giant snake. These beliefs mean that many places are sacred to the aboriginals. Rock paintings often show the animals that aboriginal people hunted long ago. High prices are now paid for paintings by some of today's aboriginal artists.

Traditional aboriginal ceremonies usually include singing, dancing and music played on wind and percussion instruments. For example, a didgeridoo is a carved wooden wind instrument that blows loud and deep notes.

Aboriginal dancers.
- *A traditional aboriginal dance.*
- *A festival of aboriginal song and dance is called a corroboree.*

The 'western' arts

Most Australians enjoy the same kind of arts and performances as people in other 'western' countries. Opera and other music and drama events are performed in the Sydney Opera House and in other theatres around the country. There are art galleries with paintings from the nineteenth century showing scenes from the early days of European settlement in Australia.

TV 'soap' dramas, such as *Home and Away* and *Neighbours,* show scenes from Australia to people all over the world. Films made in Australia have included the *Mad Max* films with Mel Gibson. The Paul Hogan film *Crocodile Dundee* showed the grasslands and swamplands of Northern Territory.

National and local events

National Australia Day is celebrated on 26 January and Anzac Day on 25 April. Anzac Day is a reminder of the many Australian and New Zealander soldiers who were killed during World War 1.

There are many local festivals, such as the 'Essenfest' food and drink festival in the Barossa Valley. Some of these festivals were brought to Australia by immigrants from the UK, Germany and other countries. In Northern Territory, there is a public holiday on 1 August, called Picnic Day. Perhaps the strangest festival is the annual 'Henley on Todd' boat race in Alice Springs. The Todd river is bone dry at that time of year so competitors have to run, carrying their boats.

The Sydney Opera House.
- *This is on the waterfront near the city centre.*
- *The unusual roof looks like sails on a yacht.*

The Anzacs were soldiers from Australia and New Zealand, who fought in the Gallipoli campaign during World War I.

AUSTRALIA FACTFILE

Area 7,682,848 square kilometres

Highest point Mount Kosciusko 2229 m (on the mainland)
Highest point on Australian territory: Mawson Peak on Heard Island in the Southern Ocean

Climate

	January temp.	July temp.	Total annual rainfall
Sydney	22°C	12°C	1214 mm
Darwin	28°C	25°C	1661 mm
Alice Springs	28°C	12°C	252 mm

Population 18.1 million

Population density 2 people per square kilometre

Life expectancy female 80, male 74

Capital city Canberra

Population in towns and cities 82%

Population of the main cities (millions)
Sydney	3.7
Melbourne	3.1
Perth	1.2
Adelaide	1.1
Brisbane	0.8

Land use
Grass	54%
Forest	14%
Crops	7%
Other	25%

Employment
Services	70%
Industry	24%
Farming	6%

Main imports
Machinery and equipment
Textiles
Metals
Paper
Vehicles

Main exports
Raw materials including metal ores
Food
Livestock
Grains
Meat
Wool

Language
English	89%
Italian	2%
Aboriginal	1%
Other	8%

Religions
Christian	76%
Other and non-religious	24%

Money The Australian dollar ($A)

Wealth $US17,500
Note: This is calculated as the total value of what is produced by the country in one year, divided by its population and converted into US dollars.

GLOSSARY

aboriginal people the native people who have lived in Australia for many thousands of years

artesian basins places where there is underground water

bushwalking walking and camping in the Australian bush

capital city the city where a country has its government

consumer goods goods people buy for use in their homes

continent the largest area of land

dreamtime the time, in aboriginal beliefs, before there were people

drought a long period without rain

emigrated left one country to live in another

energy the power needed to drive machinery

exports goods that are sent out of a country

federation a group of states that are part of the same country

flash floods sudden floods caused by heavy rain

freight goods that are transported

heavy industries industries making manufactured goods such as cement and steel

hot desert a hot area where the rainfall is below 250 mm in a year

independent country a country with its own government

inland drainage an area that rivers flow into, but do not flow out again

irrigation the system of channeling water onto farmland

landforms relief features in the landscape

light industries industries making low weight, high value goods

manufacturing industries industries that produce goods in factories

marsupial an animal with an external pouch for their young

Merino sheep a breed of sheep with fine wool

mineral lines railway lines used to carry minerals such as iron ore

monolith a large hill made of a single block of stone standing on its own above a plain

penal colonies places where convicts used to be sent

plains large areas with flat relief

raw materials what goods are made from

rouseabout the name given to a general farm worker in Australia ('roustabout' in other countries)

savanna climate a tropical climate with two seasons

sheep stations very large farms for sheep in Australia

shield a large area with ancient rocks, at the heart of a continent

soil erosion the wearing away of soil

speciality shops shops that only sell one type of goods

suburbs housing areas on the edge of a city

tropical monsoon climate a hot and wet climate caused by a seasonal change in the wind direction

wilderness areas remote areas with natural vegetation

INDEX